SOUL-CRIES:

A JOURNAL

Jennie Denney

Photos by:
Jennie & Ryan Denney

You are a blessing!

love,
Jennie Denney

Dedication:

To Ryan, Peyton, Reagan, Kaitlyn and Liam.

I love you.

My Dear Reader,

There is a power behind images that brings a whole new depth of meaning to an experience. Combining images with words has a way of moving the soul to an unexplainably deeper level than if one was to just simply read the words. This book is a combination of words, images, and space for journaling, reflection, and prayer. It is meant to be used as a form of spiritual deepening through poetry, imagination awakening through imagery, and self-discovery through journaling.

May your life be ever deepened, and your spiritual journey enhanced as you read, ponder, and journal through this unique book of images, poems, and space. As you journey through, may you become increasingly aware of your own soul cries.

Thank you for allowing me to be a part of it.

Jennie Denney

TABLE OF CONTENTS

What Will They Think

Can I just crawl under a rock and die right now?

Or just hide in my room the rest of the week?

Why do I say things that shouldn't be said
Or think things that shouldn't be thought?
I'm embarrassed, mortified, ashamed, sad.
What will they think?
Who do they think I am?

Wonder

I wonder how much more brilliant the colors,

How much softer the grass

How much clearer the atmosphere will be?

I wonder

If we will be able to understand the animals?

Will the trees and flowers be able to speak?

Will they finally be able to share the stories

Of those they have watched so closely?

Will the oceans open up, revealing their secrets of lost one's at sea?

Will all this matter when this mortal body passes and I walk fully into the presence
of my Lord?

Today

Take my life and let it be

Consecrated Lord to Thee

Be my Shephard and teach me

How to be Your sheep.

I need You, Lord.

Take my second-guessing and motive-wondering

Help me to see You, follow You, and enjoy the ride.

Give me strength and courage I need today,

And help me to be open to what You have to teach me.

Ask and It's Yours

A life of exciting adventures awaits you!

A life,

Fullest of the full

Is here for the taking

Ask and I will give it to you.

No more stumbling in the dark,

taking baby steps of trust!

Take your hands off your eyes, my child

See the world all around you!

I made it for you,

for you to enjoy!

All of it for you,

Ask and it's yours.

Stretch out your arms, my child,

Feel the breeze all around you!

It's My breath whispering

Songs of love to you.

Feel the freedom

And goodness

I have to offer you,

Ask and it's yours!

COME
(From Psalm 34:8)

Come,

Taste and see the goodness of the Lord.

You are invited

To experience the wholeness the Lord has to offer.

Come,

Trust that the Lord is good,

His love endures forever.

Seek,

He is waiting for you to

Come.

The Lord

(From Psalm 36:5&6)

Your love is all around me,

May it consume my very soul.

Your faithfulness,

Permeates the very air I breathe.

May I breathe it in and rest in it.

Your righteousness is in everything I see,

May my eyes see Your goodness all around me.

Your justice,

Stretches farther than I can sense.

May I be a vessel of Your love,

Faithfulness,

Righteousness and

Justice.

Guidance

Continue to guide our steps.

Help us to wait upon You

as You guide our ways and

make our paths clear.

May this be an adventure,

May I enjoy it,

knowing it's You

Throwing open the floodgates.

God, help us to walk expectantly knowing You're right by our side.

BEYOND MEASUREMENT

Thank You for Your faithfulness;
Thank You for Your goodness;
Thank You for teaching me Your ways.
Your depth calls to my depths;
My soul is drawn to You.
Show me your ways,
Continue to guide me along Your path—for that is the way to life—
the fullest life.
May my heart beat as Yours—with a love beyond measurement.
May I see You in the hardships;
May I see You in the joy.
Show me Your ways.
Teach me Your paths.
May I depend solely on You.

May it be You

When I look up into the heavens,
What do I see?
When I gaze across the earth,
What do I want?
May my answer be You, Lord
May my heart say Jesus.
When my body starts to fade,
Who will shine through?
When my mind fails me

Who will they see?
May my heart say Jesus
May the answer be You,
May my soul cry out for You
May they see Jesus
Where is my strength?
May it be in You
Where is my portion?
May it be You

Rest

(From Psalm 84:3)

May I be like the sparrows and swallows

who have found a home,

found rest.

May I know peace is at Your feet—

Where the only true place of rest and peace is.

SURE FOOTED

May I know Your love and faithfulness are connected

And there is peace in Your love.

May I see the world around me,

The people,

Family and friends

You have brought into my life

May I see Your faithfulness

May I look up into the skies and know Your righteousness is good and holy

May I know what You have for me is good and it's best for me

May I trust You have gone before me

Preparing the way

Leading me in love

Guiding me with your truth

Clearing the path

So I can walk,

Sure-footed in your way.

UNIQUE

Thank you for being there for me
Thank you for drawing me nearer to You.
I've learned that You love me—not for what I do,
but because You made me.

You've knit me together unlike anyone else—created me uniquely,
with Your personal touches.
Not one person on this planet is the same as another—
what a beautiful example
of how vast, wide, deep and long Your love is!

Not one story is the same—each one unique and different to that
individual.
Lord, a whole new meaning
for being:
Fearfully and wonderfully made in Your image!

Grace for Myself

May I be wise enough to listen,
And slow in speech.

May I hear what's being said,
And not assume

May I be filled with grace and love;
That Your peace would overwhelm me.

May I remember to seek Your face.

May I not just have grace for others,
But by I also have grace for myself.

WAKE UP

Oh heart,

Be steadfast!

Oh soul,

Sing and make music!

Wake up!

Feel the joy,

Feel the breath of the Lord!

Be drenched with His love!

This desert of mine is parched,

I need Your holy water to consume my deepest desires

For Your love is greater

And higher

Than the skies' reach

Your mercies and faithfulness

Stretch farther than the east is from the west

The Mind

I find I am my own worst enemy:

My mind tells me such evil lies.

I believe them,

Think them,

Ponder them,

Live them.

God help me to push through.

May I believe what is good

And right.

Let it be truth and grace.

Flood yourself into my mind,

That it would be a tool for good

Not my downfall.

I find my mind is deceiving.

It lies,

Distorts truths,

Exaggerates events.

When I choose to believe it,

I move away from who I was
meant to be

The Ugly Me

You know me more than I know
myself

You've seen my dreams,

Counted my tears,

You've deciphered my motives,

Understand my fears,

You know my darkest secrets,

You know what makes me tick.

Through it all,

You still love me!

Through it all,

You still care.

You love me,

Deeper than I could ever
imagine,

You want me,

All of me.

Where can I hide from You, my
God?

Where can I escape Your
presence?

You are here with me.

Through it all—

Despite my shortcomings,

Despite what I see as the ugly me.

You love me.

You truly see all of me

And yet you still pursue me—

Gently pursue me,

Even when I hide in vain.

Oh the wonder of it all!

That you still love me

Despite what I see as the ugly me!

You call me beautiful!

You call me yours!

I praise You, Jesus!

I praise You, Lord!

QUIET

Sometimes I hear You through a song

Sometimes I feel you in the wind

Sometimes I see You in people's eyes

Mostly I sense You in the quietness of my heart.

My soul longs for these quiet moments

They are too few and far between

May I rest in knowing

That you are everywhere.

I want to feel You always

.

I want to know You are all around me

May my eyes be opened

May I rest in knowing

That You are everywhere.

Sometimes I hear You through the crashing waves

Sometimes I feel You in the warm sunshine

Sometimes I see You in the gentle rain

Mostly I sense You in the quietness of my heart

HELP

Help me to see Your goodness in all of this

Help me to see Your grace in my life

I can't see past the desert in front of me

But I know You're where I am.

WISDOM

(Taken from teachings by Jan Johnson, Keith Matthews & James Bryan Smith at the Apprentice Experience, Friends University, Wichita, KS)

Wisdom

What is wisdom?

Is it something that can be measured?

Is it something that can be had?

Wisdom

What is wisdom?

It is a holy knowledge of

what life is in the Kingdom of God

It is more often caught than taught

It is slowly grown, molded, stretched

Over a life-time of choices.

Choices to study the life of Jesus

Choices to walk with those who

have walked with Jesus longer

Choices to seek wisdom with every ounce of energy one can muster over a life-time

Choices to face the ugliness that is inside

Wisdom

This is wisdom.

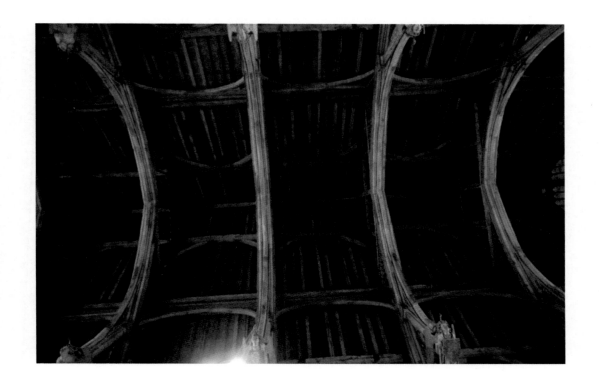

Character

May my character not be my god
May my pride not be my god
May my quest for perfection not me by god
May my search for wisdom not be my god
To replace my Lord is easy
To put on a pedestal what does not belong
Is often quick and goes unnoticed
Until it becomes too late.
May I know myself well enough
May the truth set me free –
Not bind me up
May I seek You, Lord
May I seek You, alone.

Solitude

Solitude is an interesting thing

It can either drive you mad

Or it can create space for one to dive deep into their soul

Soul searching leads one to revelations about themselves they may not want to see

This is where wisdom beacons things out of the dark

And into the light

For true healing can only happen in the light

It is our choice—

Whether to look away and live in the shame and hide those things in the dark

Or we can swallow our pride,

Look at those things,

Listen to wisdom,

Bring those things into the light

And find true healing

This is where wisdom is proved right by her deeds.

———

Reliance

(From Psalm 86)

When I rely on Your faithfulness,
I don't fear what's ahead.
When I know Your ways,
I know You are trustworthy.
When my heart is undivided,
I seek You.
When I fear Your Name,
I know You are with me--
By my side,
Walking with me,
Through this life

Peace

(From Psalm 16)

I am perfectly safe in God's Kingdom
When I rely on the Lord to sustain me,
He will provide in ways that are clear it is Him sustaining me.
The Lord counsels me at night,
Speaking words of peace and love,
Allowing me to rest in His presence
As long as I continue to live in God's Kingdom,
Trusting Him for my sustenance,
He will provide me with a peace that surpasses all understanding
Through every situation
I encounter.

Guidance

(From Psalm 13)

My heart is heavy
My soul is weary

A mixture of sorrow, fear, excitement, anxiousness
A weightiness I have never felt before

I want to cry, laugh, scream
All at the same time

Sometimes I wish you would just tell me what do to next

But maybe you have

May I walk forward
With sure steps and eyes open
Trusting Your goodness

May I seek your face and be filled with Your wisdom in these decisions

No matter what path I take

May I trust in Your unfailing love

Rejoice in what You've done for me
And sing Your praises—for You have been good to me.

Revelation

(From Psalm 17)

I pray to You

For I know You will answer me

Hear my prayer, Lord

For I know You are listening

I ask that You show me the wonders of Your great love

Help me to know what that means

I want to soak in Your great love

Help me to grasp the depth, height, width

And breadth of Your love!

Life

I woke up praying again this morning,

Asking for wisdom and guidance.

I asked for a check in my heart.

I asked for your help,

To keep my eyes fixed on You.

I asked for You to provide for a miracle.

I asked for Your peace,

For that is the only way I will have the courage to move forward.

I asked for patience,

For Your timing is perfect.

I asked for Your guidance.

I asked for wisdom,

For You lead me to life everlasting.

—

Trust

I can only see the past and present

Strengthen my trust in you

That I would live this life

Trusting You've got the future.

May I continue to remember that creating space in the day for You to speak into my life is the kind of Spiritual formation my heart and soul needs.

Help me to finish strong.

May your hand be at work in my life. May I trust Your will would be done.

Amen.

Open Eyes

With eyes open I will walk through this life

Trusting Your goodness will follow me all the days of my life

With arms open wide I will trust in Your faithfulness

Knowing You are with me

Guiding me

Every step of the way

Here's my heart,

My hopes, dreams and plans.

May they be sifted through Your love

For you know me best. better than I know myself

I need help trusting You are leading me to good pastures

Leading me to still waters

Leading me to the life You created me for.

Steady

(From Psalm 32)

Help me to live in the present
Not the past or the future
You have me here today
You know my yesterday and tomorrow
Help me to live today
Steady
Enveloped in the warmth of your loving gaze
Trusting you are walking with me
By my side
Knowing when I cannot move one step further
You pick me up and walk for me until I'm ready to walk with my own feet again
Search my heart and know me
May my eyes forever be on You.

Swamped

My mind is swamped

My soul feels heavy

I want to hear You,

But I can't seem to get my mind to stop rolling long enough to hear Your voice

My thoughts, worries, anxieties

Seem to keep drowning You out

Help me to see You are still here in the midst of the mess

Not Alone

When it's dark and I can't see
one foot in front of the other

When I'm all alone in the middle
of a crowded room

I remember:

Your faithfulness

Your love

Your goodness

Your presence

I'm not alone

When life sucks

When the onslaught of waves
become too much

When I'm up to my neck in
disasters and there's nothing to
do but look up

I see:

Your hand stretched toward me

Your face smiling at me

All the times You've walked with
me—never leaving my side

You are all around me,

Never leaving my side

You

You who created the heavens and the earth

You who placed and named every star up above

You whose seen every tear I've held back

Your Name be praised

You who knit me together

You who is great and mighty

You whose eyes see Your people

Your Name be lifted high

You who says I am loved and cherished

You who carried me in Your arms of love

You who gives me purpose

You who calls me Yours

Just

Just as God has created each

and every person uniquely in His image,

So is He vast.

Just as God has created every type of bird in the air

and tree in the ground,

So is He larger than we could ever imagine.

Just as God has created every school of fish

and species of animal,

So is His hand in all things.

Steady Me

Steady me

For I keep finding myself moving forward

Faster and faster

Not slowing down

I want to rest in the goodness You've given me now

Not run toward a hope, a dream, a vision You've promised tomorrow

Steady me

To live today and hope for tomorrow

To grow in Your grace today

not rush through today's goodness.

I want to see You work in my life today,

Knowing that tomorrow will come in time.

Steady me.

Unshaken

I want to know that when I stand
in Your goodness and grace I am
unshaken

When I rely on Your love and
affirmation

I am unmovable —

Like a tree that isn't bent by the
strong winds, my trunk is able to
withstand all sorts of

Hardships, trails, and tribulations

With roots strongly embedded in
Your truth,

Your Word,

the knowledge of Who You are

and Who You say I am

I am able to stand firm against
the waves,

wind,

storms

I am unshaken to my core

My branches might be a bit
broken

I may have lost my leaves

But my core stands strong,

proud,

humbled,

and strengthened by the storm —

Strengthened by the knowledge
that You remain, and I am

Unshaken

CHAOS

Quiet waters

Smooth surface

A gentle wave here and there

Glass

The colors of a sweet sunrise

A bird chirping

The smell of pine

Even when my soul feels
overwhelmed and sad

You remind me of Your goodness

Even when there's chaos all around

You lead me beside quiet waters

Reminding me of Your steadiness,

Refreshing my soul

A world full of chaos,

Yet a thread of hope remains

Woven throughout history

Reminding those who are willing to
see

That Your goodness will prevail.

May I Follow

May nothing I do go ahead of You

May I wait in stillness and patience

Guide me, Lord

As I seek Your face,

May my confidence in Your goodness grow

As I listen for Your voice,

May my patience remain steadfast

As You walk,

May I follow,

Humbly laying myself down.

Bring Them On

I'm not asking that You take away my burdens

For if burdens bring me closer to You,

For if burdens make me fall to my knees in front of You,

Bring them on!

I'm not asking that You make my life easy

For if hardships are what deepen my faith,

For if hardships teach me to trust You

Bring them on!

What I am asking is that You lead me through

May I feel Your presence as I walk the valleys

What I am asking is that You don't leave my side

Be with me always,

Guiding me through.

I want to walk with abandon,

Knowing You are by my side

I want to enter into Your story —to be a part of what You are doing

To redeem this world.

No Pretenses

As I watched my children play,
I was struck by what it means to be child-like.

Despite the awkward language barriers;

Despite the obvious age differences;

They played.

They laughed.

They used hand motions and what little words they knew

To communicate;

To create a game played together.

Put 10 children in one room from different parts of the world,

With no pretenses;

Nothing planned;

See what happens.

Chances are,

Something beautiful will happen

.

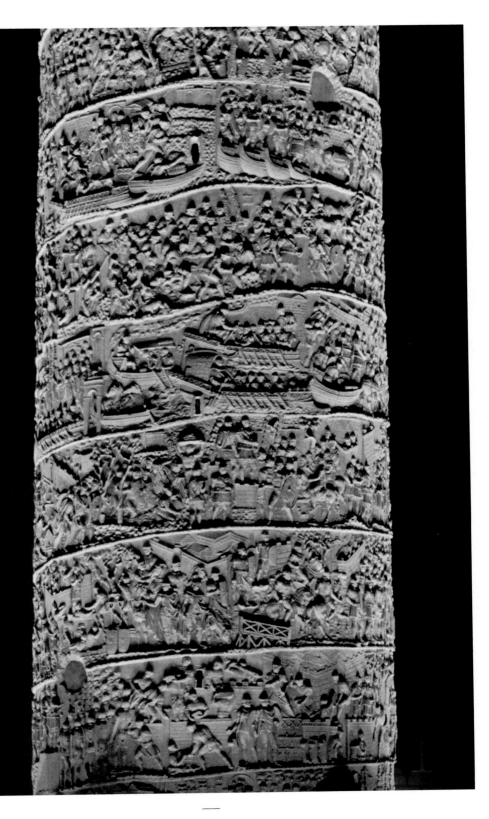

Pillar of Strength

Will You be my Pillar of Strength?
Will You guide my steps as I take them –
one by one?
Yes,
You will
And for this I praise You!

Will You still be there when I falter?
Will you remain when I look away?
Yes,
You will
And for this I remain

Enveloped in Your loving arms
Steady as an arrow
Trusting in You,
Even as I falter,
Stumble and fall.

Baby Girl

Baby girl, don't grow up too fast
This world is full of people who beckon for that

Baby girl, take your time, enjoy your innocence, rest in it

Baby girl, don't grow up too fast

This world is harsh, uncaring, cold

Baby girl, take your time

Dance, dream, play, sing, imagine, daydream, laugh, be carefree

Baby girl, you're growing up

Remember to enjoy today

Embrace your innocence

Celebrate your youth.

Learn all you can about today

So that tomorrow

When you have grown up

You can look back and be confident in who you have become

Baby girl, I celebrate who you are

And who you're becoming

You're beautiful, smart, strong, courageous

As you ready to step into this cold, dark world

May you be a beacon of light that draws those around you to the One Who Has brought light to this world.

UPWARD

Revive my soul
For I am weary and worn

Encourage my spirit
For my hopes are dwindling

May my eyes continue looking upward
So my heart doesn't sink into despair
Revive my soul

For I am weary and worn

Breathe a fresh breath into my depths
That I may feel Your re-energizing spirit within me

Lift me up
Carry me through
Help me to know You're where I am

Holder of the Chisel

Encased in hard sediment I find I have been molded,

crafted and shaped by this world.

Words of hatred, words of scorn, lies I've believed about myself,

Layers of open wounds and ugly scars

I have hidden away deep inside my heart.

Deeply encased in this hard sediment

My soul has cried out for freedom.

It has longed to dance without shame

It has longed to sing without fear

It has longed to experience its truest self

Yet it remains hidden,

Stuck

Behind the molded mask.

There is a lie deeply hidden within me,

A lie that breathes deeply inside me.

A fear that if the sediment is to be chipped away

if that molded mask falls away,

I will be naked

laughed at, made fun of, not good enough.

All those words of scorn and hatred I have chosen to believe

will be revealed as true.

I could never face that pain.

So, I remain, comfortably hidden behind my mask of plaster,

refusing the pain of the chisel.

The muffled cry of my soul

is more bearable than the pain I fear

will come if I allow that chisel to come near.

There are times, though, when

that soul-cry for freedom breaks through

It begins with a drumbeat

in the background that won't stop.

When I finally pause to hear it, I choose to ignore it

When ignoring it falters, I begin to distract myself.

Those distractions grow as that annoying drumbeat won't stop.

It continues getting louder and louder

Those distractions become less and less satisfying until I finally look and scream:

"WHAT!"

I see that chisel aiming right at my heart

I scream and groan in agony

I writhe in anxiety

That chisel comes closer,

eventually making contact

with the very part of me I have chosen to hide.

The pain is so much more than I feared

I hold my chest, fall to the earth beneath me, writhing.

I open my eyes for a second, seeing the piece that was chipped off of me,

I stretch out my arm, and I cry out, realizing it is just out of my reach.

Memories bombard my mind

Deeply wounding

Memories long hidden away

Those of rejection and mistreatment

Tears flood my eyes

I weep, deep heaving, soul wrenching tears

I wail in agony as that horrible ugly scar is re-opened,

oozing out its horrid, putrid contents

It's devastating.

My energy spent, the tears subside

I find the chisel gone.

I dry my eyes, wipe my nose

and I look up.

There's something new, something different.

I look down where that wretched chisel met my mask

I see a pale new skin in place of the hardened sediment.

There's a small warmth inside of me

I feel I can breathe for the first time.

For the first time I can think on that memory

rather than feeling the pangs of shame

I oddly feel what can only be described as

peace.

I lay my head back and rest,

no longer desiring to reach for that piece of sediment

I once thought I needed so desperately.

Is this peace,

this glimpse of me

worth the suffering the chisel brings?

In the moment,

I believe so.

As time wears on, though, and I become accustomed to that new-found freedom offered by the chisel,

I forget.

I choose to remember the writhing agony over the glorious freedom.

After a while the freedom cry of my soul begins to beat again.

I'm paralyzed with fear because the memories of the pain and anguish of that initial chiseling are just too overwhelming for me to bear.

I attempt to distract myself again until that drumbeat drowns out all that is around me.

I fall on my face, protecting my heart with my hands,

Expecting that same anguishing punishment again.

This time, though, is different.

I feel a little knock on my heal—

I open my eyes and see the chisel move away.

There lays a piece of sediment, nicked from my right foot.

A few memories enter my mind,

But this time, the memories are painful, not anguishing.

These memories bring me sadness, not debilitating numbness.

I dry the few tears I shed with my hand and look down at my heal.

I see a small white scar where that sediment once lay.

I breathe a deep breath and I feel lighter.

I smile, thankful that this time wasn't as invasive as the last.

I realize that the Holder of the Chisel knew what I needed.

I needed to be reassured that not every crack of the chisel would be as painful as the last,

But each one is necessary if one's soul is going to find the freedom it longs for.

The Holder of the Chisel heard my soul's freedom cry,

Even when I refused to hear it.

He knew exactly how, when, and where to connect the chisel to the sediment I was encased in.

Little by little that sediment is chipped away.

Some pieces are larger than others,

Some more excruciating than before,

but each one necessary.

I don't know when it started,

But I have begun asking that chisel to remove parts of the sediment I feel need to be removed.

Each time it comes,

I wince in expectation,

But I have grown to realize that the freedom that chisel has to offer is greater than the comfort of being encased in that sediment.

Every once and a while the Holder of the Chisel decides on a different area that I want chiseled;

He views it as more necessary than the one I am pointing to.

This leads me to anguish and pain again,

But I know,

 and I can trust now,

That it will all lead to more freedom.

Even now, I sometimes find myself reaching for that fallen sediment,

Believing the mask it promises is safer than what is hidden beneath,

But once that small white scar appears,

I know I can trust and rest

In the gentleness and wisdom of the Holder of the Chisel.

Made in the USA
San Bernardino,
CA